To all those who have had to stop
and catch their breath

Frankie Goes to Camp

An Inspiring Tale About Learning to Breathe

Written by
Kaitlyn Shrum

Illustrated by
Kiran Akram

Frankie had a big problem. He was a mouth breather. While all of his friends would play with their lips closed and breathing through their noses, Frankie could only watch.

Frankie would stand alone, watching the other kids run fast and play for hours. Everytime he tried to keep up, Frankie would start panting, breathing so hard his tongue would hang out and his heart would race. It was no fun having to rest while everyone else was having fun.

Frankie tried to breathe through his nose, but it was always so stuffy. His mom and dad would try to help him blow it. Frankie would huff and puff, but those boogies were stuck. It was so frustrating! Summer was starting and Frankie wanted to keep up with his friends, running, swimming, and playing. He just couldn't catch his breath.

The night before summer vacation, Mom said she had a surprise. Was it a new skateboard? Maybe it was a videogame he could play inside! As Frankie waited anxiously Mom pulled out his suitcase. "Surprise! You're going to Camp Inspire! It's a camp for kids like you, who want to be better breathers."

?

That night in bed, Frankie's heart pounded and his breathing got faster. What if learning to breathe better was hard? Or even worse, scary?

The next morning, Frankie's parents dropped him off at camp. Frankie didn't know anyone. He stood there mind racing, tongue out, breathing fast. Frankie tried to catch his breath, but he couldn't. He felt like a heavy weight was sitting on his chest. Just when he thought he couldn't take it any longer, Frankie felt a gentle tap on his shoulder.

"Hiiiiiii there. I'm counselor Steeeeeve. It looks like you could use some help slooooowing down."
"Oh, yes please!" said Frankie.
"You're in luck, sloooow breathing is my speciclty. Start by putting your tongue on the roof of your mouth. It's called your palate. Close your lips and take a long, slooow breath in through your nose for 3 seconds and then sloooowly out through your nose for 3 seconds. Pretend you're filling your belly like a balloon and slowly letting the air out."
Frankie did it once, but he still felt anxious.

"Alright Frankie, let's keep using sloooow breaths as we walk to your cabin. The first activity is about to start."
Frankie started to feel a little bit better the more slow breaths he did.

Frankie was still nervous walking into his cabin, but using slow breaths helped.

The door opened and a big smile spread across Frankie's face. The other campers were a lot like him. Some had their mouths open, some had their tongues out, and some looked even more nervous than he did.

"Welcome to Camp Inspire! I'm counselor Ellie and I'm going to teach you all about the nose." A few sniffs and snorts could be heard around the cabin. "Did you know our noses were meant for breathing and our mouths for eating? Our noses help warm and filter the air we breathe."

"Our tongues should be suctioned up on our palates, lips closed, and we should be breathing through our noses," said Ellie.
Frankie tried to breathe through his nose, but it was too stuffy. After a few tries his mouth would pop open. How frustrating!

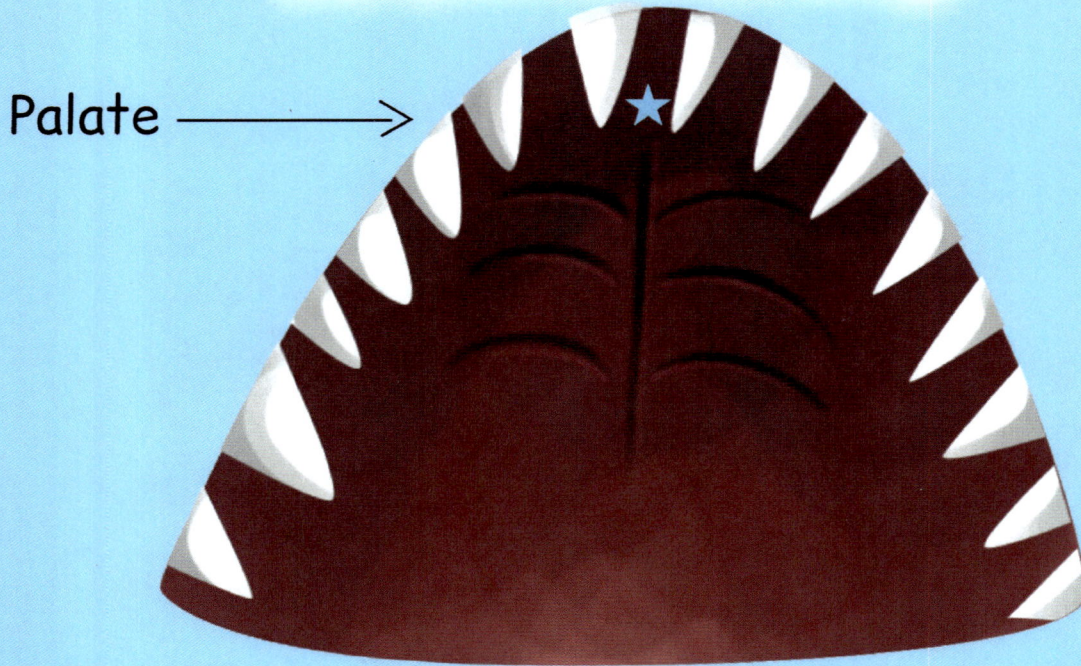

Palate ————>

Ellie noticed Frankie and some of the other campers struggling. "I think we might have some stuffy noses in the room. Let's clear them out!" exclaimed Ellie.

"First take a tissue and cover your nose. Make sure your lips are closed. Next, use one finger to close off one nostril. Take a breath in, blow out hard, and wipe. Then do it again on the other side. Keep going until all those boogies are gone!"

Frankie blew both sides once, then twice. He closed his lips and took a big breath in. Frankie's nose was actually clear and he could breathe!

As he was practicing his nasal breathing, Frankie heard a faint buzzing sound fly by.
"Hi campers, I'm Bennie! I'm going to teach you a neat trick to get those noses even less stuffy!" Frankie and the other campers listened intently. Bennie was still buzzing. But wait! He wasn't buzzing, he was humming.

"Humming can help our bodies relax and get oxygen faster and more effectively," Bennie explained. "Everyone take a breath in through your nose and hum your favorite tune while you exhale. Keep breathing and humming until you get to the end of your favorite song." Everyone was smiling and humming and the cabin sounded like a buzzing beehive.

As Frankie continued to hum and gently breathe through his nose, he realized he felt different. He certainly looked different without his mouth wide open and his tongue not hanging out. But, it was more than just his outside. Frankie finally didn't feel nervous or anxious. The world around him was quiet. He was relaxed!

Hmm mm

As everyone's tunes faded, another counselor took the floor. "Great humming everyone! I'm George. Now that our noses are nice and clear, I'm going to show you what gorillas do best." "Beat your chests and get angry!" yelled one of the campers.

"Well sort of," laughed George. "We're going to do some light chest taps and learn zone breathing."

"Zone breathing, what's that?" asked Frankie. "Our body has different breathing zones. The first zone is our diaphragm or belly area. That's the first place we want to inflate when we take a breath in through our noses. If you are relaxing or hanging out, that's the zone that should be working. But, if you are running or playing, we want to use all three zones."

"The second zone is our ribs. We want to see them expand front to back, side to side, and up and down. The third zone is our chest. It's the last place we want to inflate when we inhale," explained George.

Frankie was confused. It felt like every time he took a breath in the only thing that moved was his chest.

Zone 3

Zone 2

Zone 1

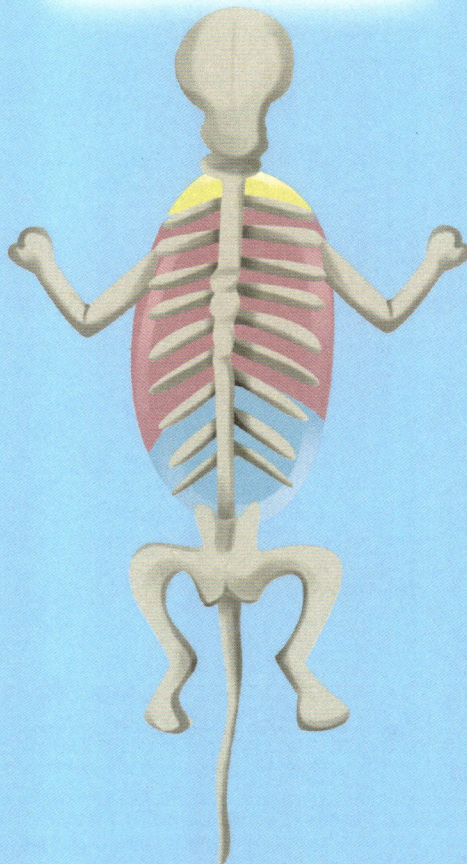

Just when Frankie thought he was getting the hang of this breathing thing, he felt like he was starting back at the beginning.

"It's ok to be frustrated, but let's try again," said George. "Try holding a paw on your belly and picture inflating it like a balloon."

"Let's try another trick to get our zones to expand more. Make your paws and hands into fists and do light gorilla chest taps, moving up and down your zones," George said excitedly.

Frankie and the other campers began tapping. Everyone's body looked looser and more relaxed. Frankie's tongue was up, his lips were closed, and he was breathing through his nose. As he kept going, Frankie saw his belly inflate and his ribs start to move. He'd never felt like he had this much breath!

"Time to put that zone breathing to the test! Let's race to the beach!" yelled George. Frankie took off with the other campers. He focused on using his nose to breathe into the zones. Frankie couldn't believe it. He didn't feel like he had to stop to pant or catch his breath! Frankie may not have been the fastest camper, but he felt great. For the first time, he was able to keep up with his friends.

Frankie got to the beach to see a giant, pointy horn poking out of the water. "A unicorn!" someone shouted. The biggest counselor yet waded onto the beach. He wasn't a unicorn at all. He was a narwhal! "Welcome to the beach campers. I'm Nick, here to teach you all about breath holds. After all, I'm an expert since I can hold my breath for 25 minutes at a time." "Twenty five minutes!" said Frankie worriedly. "Don't worry, we are only doing mini breath holds to help us relax. You've all had a busy day," explained Nick.

"Find a sandy spot. We're going to do something called box breathing," said Nick.
"I don't want to sit in a box!" proclaimed one camper.
Nick laughed, "Don't worry, there are no actual boxes in box breathing."

"We're going to trace a box in the sand as we breathe in for 4 seconds, hold that breath in for 4 seconds, breathe out for 4 seconds, and then hold for 4 seconds." Frankie gave it a try. Just like the other exercises, box breathing was a little tricky at first, but after a few minutes, it got easier.

"Keep going until you feel nice and calm. Then you have free time until lights out. Be sure to use your new breathing tricks while you play," said Nick

After a long day, Frankie lay in bed, with his tongue up, lips closed, and breathing through his nose. For the first time in a long time, his body felt great and his thoughts weren't racing. He was calm and happy. Most of all he couldn't wait until tomorrow.

"If I keep practicing, I'll finally be able to keep up with my friends," Frankie thought dreamily. Not a snore or grunt could be heard as all the campers drifted off to sleep.

THE END

Made in the USA
Las Vegas, NV
29 January 2025

17190980R00021